As Good as Anybody

Martin Luther King Jr. and Abraham Joshua Heschel's
Amazing March Toward Freedom

by Richard Michelson · illustrated by Raul Colón

Dragonfly Books   New York

For anybody and everybody marching for social justice,
and for Jennifer—walking the walk.
—R.M.

For David,
long-distance Starship Trooper.
—R.C.

Text copyright © 2008 by Richard Michelson
Cover art and interior illustrations copyright © 2008 by Raul Colón

All rights reserved. Published in the United States by Dragonfly Books, an imprint of Random House
Children's Books, a division of Random House, Inc., New York. Originally published in hardcover in the United States
by Alfred A. Knopf, an imprint of Random House Children's Books, a division of Random House, Inc., New York, in 2008.

Dragonfly Books with the colophon is a registered trademark of Random House, Inc.

Visit us on the Web! randomhouse.com/kids

Educators and librarians, for a variety of teaching tools, visit us at RHTeachersLibrarians.com

The Library of Congress has cataloged the hardcover edition of this work as follows:
Michelson, Richard.
As good as anybody / by Richard Michelson ; illustrated by Raul Colón. — 1st ed.
p. cm.
ISBN 978-0-375-83335-9 (trade) — ISBN 978-0-375-93335-6 (lib. bdg.) — ISBN 978-0-385-75388-3 (ebook)
1. King, Martin Luther, Jr., 1929–1968—Juvenile literature. 2. Heschel, Abraham Joshua, 1907–1972—
Juvenile literature. 3. Civil rights workers—United States—Biography—Juvenile literature. 4. African Americans—
Biography—Juvenile literature. 5. Jews—United States—Biography—Juvenile literature. 6. Friendship—
United States—Case studies—Juvenile literature. 7. African Americans—Relations with Jews—Juvenile literature.
8. African Americans—Civil rights—History—20th century—Juvenile literature. 9. Civil rights movements—
United States—History—20th century—Juvenile literature. 10. United States—Race relations—History—
20th century—Juvenile literature. I. Colón, Raul. II. Title.
E185.97.K5M44 2008 323.092—dc22 2007042279

ISBN 978-0-385-75387-6 (pbk.)

MANUFACTURED IN CHINA

10 9 8 7

First Dragonfly Books Edition

I solemnly pledge to uphold the fair
name of Jews. Not only because we need
their friendship, and surely we do, but
mainly because bigotry in any form is
an affront to us all.

—Reverend Martin Luther King Jr.

One hundred years ago, the emancipation
was proclaimed. It is time for the white
man to strive for self-emancipation, to set
himself free of bigotry.

—Rabbi Abraham Joshua Heschel

Martin was mad at everyone.

It was hot in Georgia and Martin wanted to swim in the pool, but the sign said WHITES ONLY.

Martin was thirsty, but the sign said WHITES ONLY.

Martin needed to pee. WHITES ONLY.

He marched to his father's church and stomped his feet.
"What good is stepping on bugs?" Daddy King said. "You're
looking down when you should be looking up."

Martin's father had an answer for everything, and that made Martin proud. Daddy King was a preacher, and every Sunday it seemed half of Atlanta crowded into the Ebenezer Baptist Church.

"The way things are," his father preached, "is not the way they always have to be. In the next world, people of all colors will live together and respect each other."

Martin didn't want to wait for the next world, but he couldn't stay angry.

Martin raced to catch the bus. He was lucky to find the last empty seat. "Stand up, boy," the driver ordered as a white child rushed on. The joy drained out of Martin's face. He wished he had walked all the way home.

Martin's mother closed her eyes and turned her head from side to side like she was reading a book she knew by heart. "Some ignorant white people think they are better than colored people," she said, hugging Martin close. "But don't you ever forget that you are just as good as anybody!"

Martin grew up and became a minister like his dad. "The way things are," he told his congregation, "is not the way they always have to be. Don't ever forget that you are just as good as anybody!"

Word spread about Martin's sermons. Some Sundays it seemed that half of Montgomery, Alabama, crowded into his little church. But sometimes Martin still got angry.

That winter a colored woman refused to stand and move to the back of the bus so that a white man could sit down. She was arrested and sent to jail.

"The time has come for action," Martin told his congregation. "Don't ride the buses until we can sit wherever we please."

Some people had to start walking in the middle of the night to get to work on time. Martin marched with them to give them courage. The bus drivers laughed. "This won't last long," one said, honking at an old lady with a cane.

"My feet is tired," she called out after him, "but my soul is rested."

One whole year passed. The bus drivers stopped laughing. They were losing money and now *they* were angry.

Finally, the United States Supreme Court changed the law.

Now Martin was able to sit up front.

But as the bus traveled through the city park, he saw a familiar sign: WHITES ONLY.

For ten years, Martin marched all over the country, speaking out for equal rights.

The Ku Klux Klan and other hate groups jeered and spat at him, but he kept marching.

Mayors and governors and judges tried to stop him from helping Negroes to vote, but he kept marching.

Sometimes Martin was discouraged, but he kept marching.

Martin organized a protest march from Selma to Montgomery. "Decent people know that prejudice is wrong," he said, "but many are too frightened to speak out."

Six hundred Negroes joined Martin, but the police blocked their way and attacked them with dogs and clubs.

Martin did not give up. "We cannot walk alone," he said, "and we cannot turn back."

He put out a call for all of God's children to join the march.

A man named Abraham answered Martin's call.

Years earlier, across the Atlantic Ocean, young Abraham strode through Warsaw, Poland, with his head held high. "Walk like a prince, not a peasant," his father had told him. "We are all God's children. You are as good as anybody."

"Are you going to be an important rabbi like your father?" his neighbors asked. Abraham nodded and answered their questions about Jewish law and customs.

"Such a scholar," his father said, smiling. "But even the Lord rested. Put down your prayer books and pass out some coins."

Abraham's family lived on donations from the congregation. Every day, poor as they were, Abraham gave away all the money left over after his mother bought groceries. "I hate poverty but I love the poor," his father said, slipping the last coin into his son's hand. "We can always find someone in greater need than ourselves."

Abraham was proud of his father, and together they prayed and studied. His father pretended to be surprised when Abraham found candies hidden between pages of the Torah. "Learning is a sweet delight, Abraham."

But sometimes Abraham found himself staring at the
sunset instead of studying. In private, he wrote poems
thanking God for the beautiful flowers and trees.

Abraham grew up and became a rabbi like his father. He also attended the university in Berlin, Germany. But as busy as he was, Abraham still found time to take long walks through the city, and to write poetry.

After he graduated, Abraham got an important job in a school, but an evil man named Hitler was appointed leader of Germany and changed the laws. Jews were no longer allowed to go to school or to vote. One evening, as he prepared for class, someone banged on Abraham's door.

"No Jews allowed in Germany," a policeman yelled. "Go back to where you came from. You have one hour to leave."

Abraham was angry. He tried to buy food for his journey.
But the sign said NO JEWS ALLOWED.

He headed to the library to return his books. But there
was a bonfire out front. JEWISH BOOKS.

Abraham took the train to Poland. He was crowded into a railroad car with hundreds of other Jews. There was no room to sit down.

When Abraham arrived in Warsaw, he was tired and hungry and cold. He stomped his feet outside his childhood home.

His mother threw her arms around him. "Perhaps in the next world, people everywhere will live together in peace," she cried.

Abraham held her close. He could feel how thin she had become. He didn't want to wait for the next world. He wished he could help her *now*.

Abraham looked for a job.

Help Wanted, the signs said.

But underneath: NO JEWS.

In America, he'd heard, everyone was treated fairly. He
would travel across the ocean, become a teacher, and send
money back home.

After months of preparation and twelve days at sea, Abraham rejoiced to see the Statue of Liberty, but his joy was short-lived. Hitler soon invaded Poland. Most of Warsaw's Jews, including Abraham's mother and three of his sisters, were killed.

Abraham marched all over America speaking out for peace and equal rights. Wherever he saw injustice, he reminded people of the beauty of life. "God did not make a world with just one color flower," he said. "We are all made in God's image."

The Ku Klux Klan and other hate groups jeered and spat at him, but he kept marching. "It is important not only to protest evil, but to be seen protesting," he told his friends. "Words must be followed by deeds."

Sometimes Abraham was discouraged. The United States had welcomed him but was not letting many Negroes vote. Abraham heard about a march for voting rights in Alabama. Should he join that protest against the government?

Abraham remembered his home in Poland. No one had come to the aid of his family.

"How can we love our neighbors," he asked, "if we abandon them in their time of need?" Abraham's faith required him to help those in greater need than himself. He knew he must answer Martin's call.

On March 21, 1965, in Selma, Alabama, Abraham Joshua
Heschel and Martin Luther King Jr. prayed together. Then
Martin stomped his feet and Abraham stomped beside him.
The time had come for action. The white man and the
black man joined hands. The Jew and the Christian joined
hands. Three thousand people stood behind them, cheering.

There were not enough police in the state to hold the marchers back. There were not enough mayors and governors and judges to stop them.

Martin took a step forward.

Abraham took a step beside him.

"This too is God's work," Abraham told Martin. "I feel like my legs are praying."

Four days later, when Abraham and Martin arrived in Montgomery, 25,000 people of all colors and religions had joined their march.

Four months later, the President of the United States signed the Voting Rights Act. It became the law of the land.

Two and a half years later, on January 11, 1968, Martin spoke at Abraham's sixty-first birthday party. He called him "one of the truly great men of our day and age, a truly great prophet."

Three months later, on April 4, 1968, Martin was shot and killed. He was preparing to march alongside garbage collectors demonstrating for job safety and equal wages in Memphis, Tennessee. He was thirty-nine years old.

Abraham spoke at Martin's funeral. "God sent Martin Luther King to us. His mission is sacred. . . . I call upon every Jew to share his vision."

Four and a half years later, on December 23, 1972, Abraham died in his sleep.

In the next world, Abraham and Martin have finally found freedom.

In this world, their family, friends, and followers are still marching.